David Adam was born in Alnwick, Northumberland. He was Vicar of Danby in North Yorkshire for over 20 years, where he discovered the gift for writing prayers in the Celtic pattern. His first book of these, *The Edge of Glory*, achieved immediate popularity. He has since published several collections of prayers and meditations based on the Celtic tradition. His books have been translated into various languages, including Finnish and German, and have appeared in American editions. Recently David retired from being Vicar of Holy Island, where he had taken many retreats and regularly taught school groups on prayer. He now continues this work and his writing from Waren Mill in Northumberland.

Music of the Heart

New psalms in the Celtic tradition

———

David Adam

Illustrations by
Monica Capoferri

First published in Great Britain in 2004 by
Society for Promoting Christian Knowledge
Holy Trinity Church
Marylebone Road
London NW1 4DU

British Library Cataloguing-in-Publication Data

A catalogue record for this book is available from the British Library

ISBN 0-281-05220-4

1 3 5 7 9 10 8 6 4 2

Typeset by Wilmaset Ltd, Birkenhead
Printed in Great Britain by
Bookmarque Ltd, Croydon, Surrey

Contents

I will sing to the Lord as long as I live;
I will make music to my God while I have my being.
Psalm 104.33

Introduction

To remain in touch with our God we have to keep in touch with the realities of the world. If our approach to the world is wrong, we will not have a right approach to God. It is also true to say that if our relationship with God is a poor one, we will not have a rich relationship with the world. The way to a healthy and full life is to make sure we do not lose contact with our God or the realities around us. We need to be aware of the world around us, its mystery and its awesome qualities. The Celtic Christians had a lovely expression for keeping in contact with the real world; they called it 'playing the five-stringed harp'. The five strings are our five senses: sight, hearing, touch, taste and smell. We are asked to use all our senses in our dealings with the world and our lives. Usually sight and hearing are the two most used of the senses but all are there to be used. When our senses are finely tuned we become aware of the wonder and mystery of our universe.

To remain in touch with anyone we need to converse, or write, at least occasionally. You cannot know someone you never talk to, you can only know *about* them. I am afraid that many people talk about God, and not so many *to* him. People theorize about God instead of having a relationship with him. My plea is that you start talking to him. Make it a habit that you get into, talking to God each day. Talking to God and learning to listen to him is the only way to get to know him. Some of the greatest examples of people talking to God are the Psalms from the Old Testament. The Psalms have been used in worship and to express people's feelings for around 3,000 years. In the Psalms we get people expressing their joys and their sorrows; they bring their hopes and their fears to God. Some psalms are from people who have a purpose and know where they want to be, but others are from people who are confused and totally lost. These psalms have sometimes been described as psalms of orientation and disorientation. Added to these two groups there are those spoken by people finding a new way, a new direction; these we call psalms of reorientation.

Under these three groupings you can find a psalm that will fit any occasion of your life, though it is better that you use them to find your own words to speak to God. Some psalms are full of joy, some of deep groaning; others have deep silences that we cannot put into words. There are times when we can only be still before creation, before a loved one, and before our God. Words fail to capture the depths of our experience.

The word 'psalm' simply means 'song' in the original Hebrew language. It was not a word to denote 'religious song'. The Hebrews made no division between religious and non-religious; for them everything was made by God and should speak of him. All of life belonged to God. In the same way, all of the human being was of God. God is interested in the body as much as in the soul, because they are a unity and one cannot function without the other. Such beliefs give the Psalms an earthiness that much of modern Christianity seems to be afraid of: this earthiness is part of our very existence. To disparage the earth is to disparage its creator. If we have a wrong relationship with the world, we will have a wrong relationship with God.

For almost fifty years I have read the Psalms from the Bible daily in Morning and Evening Prayer. For most of this time, I have read the Psalter through every month. The Psalms have influenced my thought patterns and my use of words. Added to the Psalter, I have read *The Poems of the Western Highlanders* (G. R. D. McLean, SPCK, reprinted in 2002 as *Celtic Spiritual Verse*) regularly for over forty years. These poems are the prayers and songs of a people who were deeply aware of God in their daily lives. There are prayers for travelling, milking, sea-going, sleeping, rising – in fact for every part of their lives. I feel that we would benefit from learning similar prayers for our daily lives. We cannot just use prayers from a remote farming community, or a distant culture; we need to make prayers that meet our needs today. We need to make prayers of our own.

The prayers and psalms in this book are my own attempt, in good and bad times, to keep in contact with my God. I made it a rule to write at least one prayer or psalm each day. I kept a prayer diary. Every day did not produce a work of art – that was not the idea. Some days only God and I knew what it was about. Each morning or evening, with my pen, I made personal contact with my God, the Creator, Redeemer and Sustainer of all. This contact with God is what the Scriptures call faith, for faith is a personal relationship, not a set of credal statements. Because this is about a natural relationship, it suffers, like all human relationships, from moods and ups and downs. We need to learn that God is faithful even when we are not! He is always present, waiting for us to return to him, even if we have ignored him or distressed him. God at all times waits to welcome us if only we would turn around.

St Paul tells us to 'be filled with the Spirit, as you sing psalms and hymns and spiritual songs among yourselves, singing and making melody to the Lord in your hearts' (Ephesians 5.19). This is very good advice, though we must make sure our music is directed to God – sometimes I am glad of someone who will listen to my poor singing! If we have a heart that sings it cannot be always sad, though I do know, and need, some sad songs. It is good to have words at hand that express your feelings. Yet, we also need to heed the psalmist, who says, 'Sing to the Lord a new song, for he has done marvellous things' (Psalm 98.1). We need to learn to approach God with words of our own, with our own feelings and our limitations. This book has been written to lead you into writing your own prayers and psalms, not to replace them.

Though I have divided the book into sections – Singing, Seeking, Sorrowing, Straying, Saved and Seasonal – many of the psalms and prayers could fit more than one section. Every day of our lives we belong to not one but most of these groups. I have tried out many of the prayers with groups and friends, and hope they will be of benefit to others. Having used this book, I hope you will be encouraged to keep your own prayer diary and write your own prayers and songs to God.

David Adam

Singing

SINGING

Come before his presence with a song.
Psalm 100.2

SING OF HIS LOVE

Come, praise God, sing of his great love:
Join with me and give thanks to the Creator.
It is our God who has made the earth:
He is the maker of sea and sky.
All creatures come from his love:
There is nothing that he has not made.
Come enjoy God in his creation:
Praise him for the wonders of the world.
Praise him for the smallest atom:
Proclaim his glory in the greatest star.
Give praise for the breath of life:
That the Spirit of God flows in each creature.
Rejoice that he made us out of love:
He looks after us with everlasting love.
In our God all that there is exists:
Great and mighty is his nature.
Come praise our God, sing of his love:
Give thanks to the Creator of your life.

GOD AROUND ME

I wrap around this human frame
The power of the Creator's Name.
The Father's might, his holy arm,
To shield this day and keep from harm.

I cover myself with God above,
I cling to the Redeemer's love.
Son's bright light to shine on me,
To protect today and to eternity.

I welcome in the morning light
The knowledge of the Spirit's might,
Watching my path and keeping guard,
Guiding me when the way is hard.

Today I bind all around me
The power of the Trinity.
The hand to hold,
The heart to love,
The eye to watch.
Today I bind all around me
The power of the Trinity.

GOD THROUGH THE DAY

God in the dawning,
God in the morning,
God through the day,
God on my way,
God at first light,
God through the night,
God ever kind,
God fill my mind.

God of strong power,
God of each hour,
God victorious,
God ever with us,
God fill my heart,
God never depart.
God abiding friend,
God at the end.

I WILL SING TO MY GOD

I will make music to my God.
My mouth shall sing his praises,
My heart vibrate with love,
My mind resound to his call,
My being beat in rhythm with his heart.
Let my whole life voice his Holy Name.

I will make music to my God.
Let the earth respond to his glory,
As the heaven of heavens acclaim him.
Let the sea and all that is in it rejoice,
And with the angels praise our Creator.
Let my whole life voice his Holy Name.

Every living creature join in harmony,
Come and worship our wonderful Maker.
Let all in unison give praise to the Christ,
Almighty One, who great atonement wrought.
Sing and glorify with every living breath,
The life-giving, indwelling Holy Spirit.

Come join with me, make music to the Lord.
Exult, glory and rejoice in his presence.
Let your whole life voice his Holy Name.

LIGHT IN OUR DARKNESS

Father, Creator of light out of darkness,
Bringing order out of chaos,
Giving life to the world,
We come before you.
Let your light shine in our lives.

Jesus, Light of the world,
Descending into our midst,
Conquering the darkness of death,
We come before you.
Let your light shine in our lives.

Holy Spirit, enlightening all peoples,
Dwelling within us and about us,
Giver of guidance and all good gifts,
We come before you.
Let your light shine in our lives.

Father of light,
Prince of light,
Spirit of light,
We come before you.
Let your light shine in our lives.

THE POWER OF GOD

God the Almighty is the power of my life:
I need not be anxious or afraid.
God is a fortress about me:
I need not be overcome.
I dwell in his presence:
Nothing can take him from me.
He hides me in his shelter:
When troubles are about me.
He offers me his help
When I am weak or distressed.
He will never leave or forsake me.
Nothing can separate me from him.
I dwell in his presence,
And he dwells in me.

LET THE MUSIC START

Saviour, Master,
Let the music start
In the very depths
Of my heart.

Saviour, Master,
Let the music flow,
Until my whole life
Is truly aglow.

Saviour, Master,
Let my life vibrate
In your presence,
Let it celebrate.

Saviour, Master,
Let my whole being sing
Praise to you, Redeemer,
Almighty King.

WE BELONG TO YOU

From you we have come,
To you we return.
God, you created us
Out of love and for your love.
We come to give our love to you.

From you we have come,
To you we return.
Christ, you redeem us
By your love and for your love.
We come to give our love to you.

From you we have come,
To you we return.
Spirit, you sustain us
With your love and for your love.
We come to give our love to you.

Loving, ever-living Trinity,
As you created us,
Redeem us,
Sustain us,
We come to give ourselves to you.

THREEFOLD PRAISE

Lord of the sunrise,
Dispeller of night,
Father of glory,
Giver of light.

Christ of healing,
Making me whole,
Christ redeemer,
Protect my soul.

Spirit of life,
Setting me free,
Spirit of power,
Full of glory.

Holy and blessed,
O glorious Three,
Honour and praise,
And worship from me.

JOY IN THE CREATOR

I rejoice, O God, that you are the maker of all:
That you are the creator of life,
The moulder of the earth,
The designer of the sea,
The shaper of the heavens,
And that you made me.

I rejoice, O Christ, Saviour of all,
That you redeemed the earth:
You came down for our salvation,
You rose for our promised glory,
You live in triumph in heaven,
And that you redeemed me.

I rejoice, O Spirit, sustainer of all,
That you give breath to all creatures:
You give talents to all peoples,
You give guidance and liberty,
You give all grace and goodness,
And that you give life to me.

I rejoice, O holy and blessed Three,
That you are present in all:
You are sustaining all,
You are with us eternally,
You are above all,
And yet you are found in me.

LIGHT OF CHRIST

Light of Christ,
Light a fire of love in my heart,
Love to my family and my friends,
Love to my neighbour and the stranger,
Love to my community and all humanity,
Love for all creation and to each creature.
Let that love burn and never be extinguished.
Let it flame out and bring warmth to others.

Light and love of Christ,
You brighten our dark days,
You warm our cold hearts,
You burn away all hatred,
You enlighten and protect us.
Light of Christ,
Light a fire of love in my heart.

CHRIST IN ALL

Christ in my working,
Christ in my rest,
Christ in my thinking,
Always my guest.

Christ in each action,
Christ in each deed,
Christ in each notion,
Meeting each need.

Christ at the beginning,
Christ at the end,
Christ at the centre,
Everlasting friend.

COME, MY LORD

Come, my Lord,
Come within.
Come, my Lord,
Shield from sin.
Come, my Lord,
In your might.
Come, my Lord,
With your light.
Come, my Lord,
From above.
Come, my Lord,
Fill with love.
Come, my Lord,
By my side.
Come, my Lord,
And abide.

HEART PRAISE

From within my heart,
Let the praise start.
Praise to the Creator,
With us each hour.
Praise to the Mighty One,
Provider of power.
Praise to the Redeemer,
Winning release.
Praise to the Saviour,
Giver of peace.
Praise to the Spirit,
Coming with love.
Praise for guidance,
Blessed Holy Dove.
Praise to our God,
Everlasting Friend.
Praise blessed Trinity,
World without end.

HIDDEN LORD

Hidden Lord,
Help us to find you.
Show yourself
To those who seek you.

Holy God,
Glory conceals you.
Wonderful God,
Creation reveals you.

King of kings,
We come to serve you.
Lord of lords,
We seek to obey you.

Abiding presence,
May we enjoy you.
Mighty God,
We ever adore you.

LET US ADORE

Let us adore the Lord.
Let our lips proclaim his praise.

He is the creator of all:
Maker of sun and moon,
Setter of the stars in order.
Let us adore the Lord.
Let our lips proclaim his praise.

He brought forth the earth:
Put in rivers and oceans,
Moulded the dry land.
Let us adore the Lord.
Let our lips proclaim his praise.

He made all green things:
The fruit-bearing trees,
The riches of harvest.
Let us adore the Lord.
Let our lips proclaim his praise.

He is the life giver:
Makes the birds to fly,
Causes the fish to swim.
Let us adore the Lord.
Let our lips proclaim his praise.

He is the Maker of all human beings:
Gives breath and life,
Gives us love to share.
Let us adore the Lord.
Let our lips proclaim his praise.

GOD IN ALL

God in each thought,
God in each deed,
God in each word,
God in each need.
God in each joy,
God in each sorrow,
God in each day,
God in tomorrow.
God in each dark,
God in each light,
God in each moment,
God in each night.
God with me now,
Closer than breath,
God in your love,
Protect me in death.

HAIL TO THE KING

Hail to the King: blessed is he.
Coming to share in our humanity.

Son of God, Prince of peace,
Son of man, who brought release.
Hail to the King: blessed is he.
Coming to share in our humanity.

Upon the cross and in the grave,
Facing our loss, coming to save.
Hail to the King: blessed is he.
Coming to share in our humanity.

Risen again, never to die,
Ascended Lord, Christ on high.
Hail to the King: blessed is he.
Coming to share in our humanity.

IN YOUR GRACE I GROW

Father,
Your love gives me life,
Your presence gives me peace,
Your grace gives me guidance,
Your holiness gives me hope.
I am safe in your love,
I abide in your presence,
I grow in your grace,
I rejoice in your holiness.
Glory to you, Father,
Ever with me.

A GLIMPSE OF GLORY

God, we get a glimpse of your glory,
In the radiance of the sun,
In the splendour of the moon,
In the mystery of the Milky Way,
In the individuality of each star.

The whole universe speaks:
It tells of a Creator to all who listen.
From the macro wonder of the galaxy
To the micro marvel of the human cell,
All God's creation speaks of great mysteries,
Inviting us to respond with wonder and awe.

Too often we fail to answer or to react,
Eyes refuse to see, ears are deaf,
And hearts have grown hard and cold.
We take all for granted, failing to wonder.
We have lost the freshness of each new day.

God still offers us a glimpse of his glory.
All things sing his praises, if we would listen:
Their vibrant tune is heard in each single atom,
The sound of music from the planets out in space.
Let our ears be opened and our hearts softened.
Let us join in their praises to our Maker and our God.

THE WORD OF GOD

The Word of God gives life,
And life in all its fullness.
The Word of God gives light to the eye,
Radiance to the whole of our inner being.
The Word of God revives the soul,
Refreshes us on our journey.
The Word of God is the resurrection,
The Way and the Door to eternal life.

Come to the Word of Life,
Come with reverence and awe.
Enjoy his abiding presence,
Rest in him in wonder and peace.

I AM LOVED

When the day is dark,
And my strength is gone,
When my work is hard,
And I cannot go on,
A new strange joy arises
Within the storm a calm.
I know that I am loved:
You keep me from harm.
I trust in your great power,
I am confident in your might.
You are with me every hour,
I am never out of your sight.

LET ME REJOICE IN YOU

As I arise today,
Make me aware of your presence,
Let me abide in your peace,
Awaken me to your power.
Let me rejoice in you.

As I arise today,
Make me aware of your love,
Let me abide in your light,
Awaken me to your leading.
Let me rejoice in you.

As I arise today,
Make me aware of your goodness,
Let me abide in your grace,
Awaken me to your glory.
Let me rejoice in you.

ONE IN HIM

All divisions are gone:
Heaven and earth are one.
Alleluia!

Nothing separates us from our God,
We dwell in him and he in us.
Christ has come down, taking our flesh,
We are raised to the highest heaven.
God has taken our nature upon him,
That we may share in his divinity.
Alleluia!

Christ beyond time, and in this moment,
Christ entering our world, yet beyond space,
Christ sharing in our mortality, yet eternal.
You have come down to lift us up.
We bow before you and rejoice in your presence.
Alleluia!

Praise to you, Triune God of love.
Praise to you, giver of all life.
Praise to you, Prince of peace.
Praise to you, indwelling Spirit.
Praise to you, holy and blessed Three.
Alleluia!

WE BELIEVE

We believe, O God above all gods,
You created all that exists,
By your love and for your love.

We believe, O God above all gods,
You redeemed the whole of creation,
By your love and for your love.

We believe, O God above all gods,
You sustain the whole universe,
By your love and for your love.

You are the fount of all creation,
You created the heavens and the earth,
You give us day and you give us night,
You give us morning and evening light.
From you all have their life, their being,
Entering every creature you give it worth,
You made the mighty and the meek,
You are Lord of the learned and the lowly.

We come before you in love and adoration.
We believe in you. We trust you. We worship you.
We believe, O God above all gods,
We come to your love, and for your love,
For you are here and with us now.

OPENING UP

Lord, open our eyes to see:
You are one with us,
You abide with us,
You walk with us,
You remain with us forever.

Lord, open our ears to hear:
You speak to us,
You guide us,
You encourage us,
You seek a relationship with us forever.

Lord, open our hearts to know:
You love us,
You give yourself to us,
You enfold us in affection,
You keep us in your heart forever.

GOD WITH US

Loving and everliving Lord,
You enfold us,
You uphold us,
You guide us,
You strengthen us,
You are in us,
You are about us,
You never leave us,
You do not forsake us,
You are with us.
    Alleluia.

COME AND ENJOY

Come, praise God, sing of his love:
Give thanks to the Creator of your life.
It is our God who made the earth:
He is the creator of the sky and the sea.
All creatures come from his almighty hand:
There is nothing that he has not made.
Come, rejoice in the glory of his creation:
Give praise to him for the wonders of the universe.
The greatest star and the smallest atom are his:
He made the tiniest microbe and the mighty whale.
He is in the brightest day and in the darkest night:
He is to be found in the heights and depths.
Give praise to him who gives the breath of life:
That the Spirit of God moves in each creature.
Rejoice that he made us out of his love:
We come from him and dwell in him.
All that exists is in the heart of our God:
Great, mighty and wonderful is his nature.
Come, praise our God, sing of his love:
Give thanks now to the Creator of your life.

YOUR HOLY PLACE

I come into your holy place:
I bow in adoration in your presence.
Let me be still and close to you:
Quieting myself before your love.
Awaken me today to your glory:
That I may rejoice in your grace.
Awaken my heart to your love:
That I may know your care.
Lord, I seek to do your will:
To meet you and serve you in others.
I come to you with people in my heart:
Let me go out to them with you in my heart.
Let me know that all places and people are holy:
May I find everywhere is hallowed ground.

GOD EVER IN ME

God in my life: my life in God.
God in my mind: my mind in God.
God in my heart: my heart in God.
God in my steps: my steps in God.
God in my waking: my waking in God.
God in my sleeping: my sleeping in God.
God in my being: my being in God.
God ever in me: I ever in God.

Seeking

SEEKING

Rejoice in the praise of his holy name;
let the hearts of them rejoice who seek the Lord.
Seek the Lord and his strength;
seek his face continually.

Psalm 105.3–4

GOD, GUIDE ME

O God, guide me with your power,
Grant me your presence,
Give me your love,
Go with me all my days.

Lord, let my eyes behold your glory,
Let my hands be gentle with your creation,
Let my mouth proclaim your goodness,
Let my feet walk in your ways,
Let my heart burn with your love,
Let my life reflect your presence and your peace.

I NEED YOU NOW

Why are you silent when I cry?
Why do you not come to answer me?
I have trusted in you every day:
I sought your hand to lead me.
Now I am alone in darkness and silence:
Why do you not come to answer me?

You seem to be so far from me:
I speak and I seek but find no peace.
Yet I affirm your loving presence:
In the same way as my ancestors trusted you.
Time and again they spoke of your salvation:
Of your mighty arm and your acts of deliverance.
They were not disappointed in their trust:
You were to them a great power and strength.
I looked and longed for your help:
Why do you not come to answer me?

Now I only find emptiness and silence:
I cannot live off history. I need you now.
People mock me because of my trust in you:
'Does he really believe that God cares for him?'
The dawn finds me gazing into the distance:
I look for a God who seems to be far off.
The day does not bring new hope or joy:
Why do you not come to answer me?

Let me know you are near and that you care:
For trouble and distress are close at hand.
Destruction descends upon me swiftly:
I am aware of my frailty and weakness.
I am being poured out completely:
My whole life is being drained away.
Lord, you know my suffering and pain:
Why do you not rise to answer me?

You alone can heal and restore me:
Am I being broken down for you to rebuild?
I am shattered for you to take me up and repair me:
The emptiness I have can only be filled by you.
This life is a desert without you:
Why do you not come to answer me?

My ear has not heard a single word:
My eyes have not seen your presence.
I have had no visions in the night:
I have had no great inspiration.
Yet you have taken me into your heart.
My heart belongs to you eternally.

GLORIOUS CREATOR

Great and glorious God,
I rejoice in your creation.
You brought the world into existence,
It was born out of your love and joy.
The sun and moon speak of your glory.
The planets and stars tell of your might.
The whole of the universe speaks of your majesty.

Why do you take notice of us, mere mortals?
We are less than specks of dust in space.
Our very earth is but a tiny piece of the creation,
And we are very small creatures upon it.
What are human beings, that you care for each one?
Why do you lavish such love on these children of earth?
You are to be found in every human, even the humblest.
Each child is full of your mystery and your power.

You have given us strength to have control in the world.
You have made us able to make or destroy your creation.
You have given us responsibility for the birds of the air.
We are accountable to you for the fish in the sea.
You have asked us to care for the forests and each creature.
You want us to love the world with the love you have for it.
In loving the world we will learn to love its creator.
Lord, teach us to rejoice in your creation and in you.

GOD WAITS

We cannot restrict our God to one building:
The very earth and heaven could not contain him.
God cannot be captured in books, for he is too mighty;
He cannot be pressed between pages like a flower.
He roams freely and comes to each one of us.
God hides within each of us, waiting to be found:
Our God waits to be discovered within his creation.
We need not travel to find him, he is close to each of us.
Come, find him in the heart of his creation.
God waits for you to turn to him.
Know he is in your heart and with you.
Discover all is in the heart of God,
And God is in the heart of all.

I LONG FOR YOU

Lord, I long for you, I look for you,
I watch for you, I wait for you.
I thirst for you, O my Lord,
Like someone in the desert seeking an oasis,
Like a wilderness beast seeking a stream.
I long for your presence,
I look for your love,
I watch for your coming,
I wait for your call.
Come, Lord, and satisfy me.
Come quench my thirst,
Come refresh and renew me.
Lord, I long for you, I look for you,
I watch for you, I wait for you.

MAKE ME AWARE

When the mists come down,
And the clouds are dark,
When my heart is cold,
And I feel totally on my own,
Lord, open my eyes to see
Your glory and deep mystery.
Warm my heart until I know
The closeness of your presence.
Awaken each sense, make me aware
Of your love and your power.
Come, Lord, enter my distress
And disperse the darkness.
Enter my confusion and unrest
With your stillness and peace.
Lord, I am lost without you.
Guide me and lead me,
Show me the way I should go.
Touch my life with your presence,
In the fog make me aware of you.

THE EYE OF GOD

God of life and light,
Lord of power and might,
Keep me in your sight,
Protect me through the night.

Lord of heaven on high,
Look upon me with your eye,
Guard me, body and soul,
Restore my life, make me whole.

You are watching over me,
Now and through eternity.
So when I do come to die,
You will raise me, Lord, on high.

KYRIES

Lord, have mercy on us,
In your power and might.
Lord, have mercy on us,
Keep us in the right.

Christ, have mercy on us,
Take away our sin.
Christ, have mercy on us,
Grant us peace within.

Spirit, have mercy on us,
Gracious Holy Dove.
Spirit, have mercy on us,
Heal us with your love.

I WAITED FOR THE LORD

I waited patiently for the Lord:
I kept silent and still.
I watched and waited for the Lord:
I quietened my heart and remained alert.
He came and filled my emptiness with love:
He filled my life with the glory of his presence.
The Lord lifted me out of darkness:
He watered the dryness of my life with plenty.
The Lord made the desert within me blossom:
He made my whole being spring into new life.
Blessed are those who seek the Lord:
Who turn to him in times of trouble.
God is ever present, close at hand:
The Lord Almighty comes to our aid.
Turn to the Lord and he will come to meet you:
Turn away from the darkness and to his light.
How can I tell you of his loving kindness?
Words fail me, they cannot capture God.
Come and experience his presence:
Turn now and delight in the Lord.
Learn how gracious the Lord is:
Rejoice in his saving power.
Come before him in wonder and awe:
Come and sing his praises eternally.

DIVINE EMPTINESS

There is an emptiness that only God can fill:
A hunger and a thirst nothing on earth can satisfy.
I thirst like a man who has drunk from the sea:
No matter how much I take, my thirst is not quenched.
I hunger for one thing after another and am not filled:
It is hard to be satisfied because of the longings within.
My mind does not settle, it takes on one thought after another:
I feel like a vagrant gathering and living off scraps.
There is restlessness and weariness in my whole being:
My heart cannot be filled, within is emptiness and loneliness.

They sell me goods I do not need to distract me.
I chase after things that are wasting my life away.
I follow programmes that give me no joy or guidance.
I eat, until I can eat no more but my being is not filled.
I drink and drink but I thirst all the more.
Lord, my whole being looks for you, longs for you.
I am created for you, Lord, and for the eternal.
Earthly things and passing events alone will not satisfy.
My heart has been designed for you and your love.
Come, my Lord, fill my life that I may enjoy all things.
Come, fill my heart that I may be satisfied with little.
Come, Lord, fill my emptiness, change me and I shall be
    changed.

GOD COME DOWN

Love as boundless as the ocean,
Joy deeper than the sea,
Peace as wide as the heavens,
Come Lord, come, have mercy on me.

You did not send an angel from above,
Or a messenger in your place,
You came down in power and love,
You came yourself to the human race.

The stars twinkled in sheer delight,
The heavenly hosts sang in the height,
For he who is the Prince of Light,
Entered into the darkness of our night.

Love as boundless as the ocean,
Joy deeper than the sea,
Peace as wide as the heavens,
Come Lord, come, have mercy on me.

TO WHOM SHALL WE GO?

To whom shall we go?
You alone are the Lord of life.

To turn away from you is to die.
To ignore you is to enter into darkness.
You are the way and the truth.
To lose you is to be confused and lost.
You alone are the Lord of life.

If we would turn to you,
You reach out to help us.
You want us to have life.
You offer us your love,
You give us yourself.
Where else could we go?
You alone are the Lord of life.

In your presence is the fullness of joy.
You are the light of the world.
In your presence are hope and peace.
You alone are the Lord of life.

Lord, we come to you.
Lord, we come.
Lord.

LET ME KNOW YOUR LOVE

Lord, let me know your love:
Let my heart feel it,
Let my mind absorb it,
Let my tongue proclaim it,
Let my eyes watch for it,
Let my spirit long for it,
Let it fill my whole being.

Lord, let me know your love:
Until I burn with love for you,
Until I am aflame with you,
Until my life reveals you,
Until my every action proclaims you,
Until I am one with you.
Lord, let me know your love.

PILGRIMAGE

Father, in my pilgrimage today,
Give me the joy of journeying.
Give me pleasure on the path,
Show me wonders on the way,
And guide me to your glory.

I ask your eye to watch over me,
I seek your hand to defend me,
I desire your love to enfold me,
I need your power to protect me,
And guide me to your glory.

Let your light lead me always,
Grant me of your goodness and grace,
Forgive my foolishness and frailty,
Heat my heart with your love,
And guide me to your glory.

Until at last I come to you,
And abide with you in glory.

AWAKE WITH THE DAWN

Anyone who has not wondered
At the dawning has died
During the night, or has never lived.
Each day should awaken us to wonder and awe,
To a fresh reverence for each creature.

Everything I touch burns with a presence.
All that I see dazzles me with its radiance.
A single sound fills my ears with its call.
Events flame in my heart, revealing Love.
How can I survive such wonder and awe?

They say I should not be so sensitive,
In allowing such glory to mix with the earth.
Lord, how can this be, for it is reality?
A handful of soil can open the eyes of the blind.
I have seen heaven and earth are one.

DO NOT DELAY

Come, my Lord, down from above,
Come, my Lord, surround me with love.
Come, my Lord, enter my heart,
Come, my Lord, never depart.
Come, my Lord, my light my way,
Come, my Lord, do not delay.
Come, my Lord, Prince of peace,
Come, my Lord, give me release.
Come, my Lord, free me from sorrow,
Come, my Lord, today and tomorrow.
Come, my Lord, shield me from strife,
Come, my Lord, protect me in life.
Come, my Lord, my dearest friend,
Come, my Lord, abide to life's end.
Come, my Lord, with each breath,
Come, my Lord, save me from death.
Come, Lord.
Come down.
Come among us.

I AM A SEEKER

Father,
I am a seeker,
I am often unsure,
I need your guidance,
I need your presence,
I need your love.

Father,
Give me joy in my journey,
Give me wonder on the way,
Give me your grace to guide,
Give me sureness in seeking,
Lead me to you.

Father,
Let your eye watch over me,
Let your hand guide me,
Let your presence protect me,
Until I come to rest before you,
Until I come at last before your face.

SET ME ON FIRE

Lord, you are my light and my salvation,
Set me on fire with love for you.
Lead me to the radiance of your presence,
Scatter the darkness within me and around,
Deliver me from the deep dark of death.
Awaken me to life eternal,
That I may glow with the fire of your love,
And rejoice in the brightness of your glory.
Lord, you are my light and my salvation,
Set me on fire with love for you.

UNAWARE

Lord,
I sought you,
Not realizing you are always with me.
I searched in books and in churches,
I searched in lectures and in sermons,
I searched the world for your presence,
Unaware that you are with me all the time.

I turned to look for you,
Not knowing you never left me.
I called for you to come,
Not heeding your constant call.
I looked everywhere for you,
Not understanding you are in all things.
I raced around, looking and searching,
While you wanted me to be still.
I searched for your dwelling place,
Forgetting you dwell in me and I in you.

Lord, how could I lose my grip,
When you hold me in your hands?
Dear Lord, help me to rest in you,
Knowing your love for me is eternal.

LORD, I TURN TO YOU

In turning away from you,
I hunger and I thirst,
I go through desert lands,
Without joy or peace.
All my work becomes hard,
And I can find no place to rest.
Everywhere is dull and grey,
For I have entered into darkness.

In turning towards you,
I find you waiting to meet me,
With your arms open wide.
You accept me with love,
In you I find rest and refreshment.
You have prepared me a feast,
There is music in my ears.
I am filled with deep joy,
I am at home and at peace.

Lord, lover of the loveless,
Helper of the helpless,
Hope of the hopeless,
Healer of the sick,
Need of all the needy,
I turn today to you.

COME AND VENTURE

Unlock the door, discard the key,
Come out and venture with me.
Forget the past, the deeds once done,
Come rise to the new day and the sun.
Carry no load, travel light,
Cast off the shadows of the night.
Go the way which none have trod,
Venture out as a child of God.
There are no maps for the road ahead,
Yet that should not fill you with dread.
The road unknown, that before you lies,
Will twist and wind until you arise.
Wherever you go throughout the land,
You are always in the Father's hand.

MAKE ME WHOLE

Lord my God, I come to you for shelter,
Save me from all that would drain and devour me.
I am afraid there is so little of me left,
I am diminished and feel very small.
I know that I am perishable goods.

Lord, make haste to help me, to rescue and restore me.
You, Lord, know my brokenness and weakness,
Come, heal me and make me whole.
You alone are my Saviour: in you I hope.
You alone are my strength: you are my God.

Sorrowing

SORROWING

How long will you forget me, O Lord, forever?
How long will you hide your face from me?
Psalm 13.1

MY SOUL WEEPS

God of earth, God of sky,
God of sea, hear my cry.

I cry out to you, my soul weeps:
I cry for the soiled and the spoiled,
For the sea birds with oil on their wings,
For the creatures lost forever, never to return.
God of earth, God of sky,
God of sea, hear my cry.

I cry out to you, my soul weeps:
For the destruction of the rain forests,
For the constant decimation of trees,
For the loss of land to the desert.
God of earth, God of sky,
God of sea, hear my cry.

I cry out to you, my soul weeps:
For the fouling of the air we breathe,
For the polluting of the environment,
For the dirtying of the seas.
God of earth, God of sky,
God of sea, hear my cry.

I cry out to you, my soul weeps:
For the homeless and the stranger,
For the hungry and the destitute,
For the tortured and the rejected.
God of earth, God of sky,
God of sea, hear my cry.

GOD IN YOUR TROUBLES

God be with you in your troubles,
Christ come and lighten your darkness,
The Spirit of God renew and refresh you,
The power of the presence be all about you,
The Almighty Three ever protect you,
The Holy One be known to be with you.

The gracious God go with you and guide you,
The love of the Lord lead you and enfold you,
God answer your heartfelt prayers and petitions,
Keep you from ill and all that would harm you,
That we may be able to rejoice at your well-being,
Knowing you are safe in the heart of our God.

HAVE MERCY, MIGHTY GOD

Have mercy, Lord, upon us,
Mighty God of grace.
Have mercy, God, upon us,
Let us see your face.

Have mercy, Christ, upon us,
Hear us from on high.
Have mercy, Christ, upon us,
May we never die.

Have mercy, Lord, upon us,
Spirit, set us free.
Have mercy, Lord, upon us,
Bring us liberty.

GOD FORSAKEN

God, why have you forsaken me?
Why leave me in this pain?
The sun is hidden from my sight:
The dark clouds drop cold rain.
The fury of the wind does not cease:
The very earth trembles and quakes.
The roaring waves increase:
The air vibrates and all shakes.
The storm gets stronger still:
A great darkness fills the sky.
Why, O God, do you keep silent?
Why, O God, I ask you why?

Do not trust your feelings:
They will lead you astray.
Trust me in the darkness:
I am a sure and safe way.
The sea will subside:
The surface will be calm.
The sun will shine again:
I will keep you from harm.
I am with you every moment:
I may be silent but I am near.
I stay with you always:
There is no need to fear.

HEAR OUR CRY

God our Creator,
God most high,
God immortal,
Hear our cry.

God all-merciful,
God most high,
God all-powerful,
Hear our cry.

God invisible,
God most high,
God ever present,
Hear our cry.

GOD, HAVE MERCY

God of light,
God of moon,
God of sun,
God of stars:
>   Have mercy.
>   Have mercy upon us.

God of wind,
God of air,
God of breath,
God of Spirit:
>   Have mercy.
>   Have mercy upon us.

God of water,
God of rain,
God of rivers,
God of seas:
>   Have mercy.
>   Have mercy upon us.

God of earth,
God of soil,
God of land,
God of all:
>   Have mercy.
>   Have mercy upon us.

INTO THE DEEP

Lord, you disturb me, unsettle me,
Moving me out of the shallows,
You draw me into the great deep.
You beckon me to the mighty sea,
Though my boat is frail and small.
You lead me away from comfort,
From safety that is like the grave.
You ask me to travel in faith,
With no apparent light to guide.
In the darkness and the danger,
You show me the stars and your love.

You disturb, unsettle me, O God,
Seeking to lead me into new life and hope.
You ask me to let go of my possessions,
To make more room in my life for you.
You seek to possess me and to fill me,
How empty my life is without you.

You disturb, unsettle me, O God,
Yet you offer me your strength and peace.
Above everything, you offer me yourself,
Your presence brings me power and relief.
You never leave me or forsake me, O God,
I rejoice in you and in your everlasting love.
Praise be to you, O God, in you I ever abide,
On the oceans of the world, whatever the tide.

OUT OF THE DEEP

Out of the deep I call to you, O God:
Out of the darkness of my night.
Out of the deep I call to you, O God:
Lord, come in your great might.

Out of the deep I call to you, O God:
Out of the depth of my own despair.
Out of the deep I call to you, O God:
Lord, I need to know that you care.

Out of the deep I call to you, O God:
Out of the turmoil of my troubled soul.
Out of the deep I call to you, O God:
Lord, come to me and make me whole.

Out of the deep I call to you, O God:
Out of my fear and utmost agony.
Out of the deep I call to you, O God:
Come, my Lord, my life, and set me free.

KYRIES

God above all gods,
Father of the universe,
Creator of all things:
>Have mercy upon us.

Light of all lights,
Redeemer of the world,
Saviour of all:
>Have mercy upon us.

Power of all powers,
Provider of all gifts,
Breath of life:
>Have mercy upon us.

Holy and blessed Three,
Glorious Trinity,
Three Persons in unity:
>Have mercy upon us.

SPEAK, LORD

Lord, why are you silent, when I am silent?
Why do you not speak to me when I am listening for your voice?
I make space for you. I make time. I hear nothing.
I know you are not there to be commanded.
I know I cannot order you to act at my request.
Lord, I need to hear your voice. I need your guidance.
I wait upon your word. I am in need of direction.
Speak, Lord, for your servant is listening. Let me hear you.
Why this silence? Why this lack of communication?
What do you mean, I should be satisfied with your presence?

Forgive me, Lord, I have been seeking presents, not the
    presence.
I have been searching for you, shouting for you, and you are
    here.
Lord, let my heart beat more in tune with your heartbeat,
Until I know that I dwell in you and you in me.
Let my will become in harmony with your will,
That my whole life may reveal you and your glory.

LORD, OPEN US TO YOU

Open our eyes, Lord, to the beauty of this day.
Open our eyes to the glory of your presence.
Open the eyes that have narrowed their vision.
Open the eyes that are clouded with familiarity.
Open the eyes that are blinded to beauty.
Open the eyes that are weary with watching.
Open the eyes that are distorted with sorrow.
Open the eyes that are unwilling to see the truth.
Open the eyes that are only able to see greyness.
Open the eyes that are selective in their seeing.
Open the eyes that are shut through fear.
Open the eyes that are closed in the sleep of death.
Lord, open the eyes of our hearts.
Enlarge our vision,
Increase our awareness,
Make us more sensitive,
Open our eyes to your presence and to you.

I WEEP FOR THE WORLD

For you, O beautiful creation,
I cry out in desperation.
I am in sorrow for oceans deep,
On the seashore I sit down and weep.
I mourn for the sea birds' oiled wings,
Plaintive curlew no longer sings.
A single oiled bird tells of our plight,
Glory and mystery are lost from our sight.
I am sad for all creatures forever lost,
In the name of trade and to keep down cost.
I weep for the forests, cut and laid bare,
I hurt for the creatures no longer there.
I cry for the steady destruction of trees,
For the loss of birds, and killing of bees.

We control all things that are under the sun,
And create a desert when we are done.
Lord, let us see that we share with the creatures,
You are revealed in their various features.
Whatever to the least thing we tend to do,
We show our relationship to the world and you.

DELIVER ME

Lord, deliver me,
Deliver my eyes from tears and my feet from falling.
Deliver me from deep darkness,
From eternal night.
Deliver me from evil,
From all that would harm.
Deliver me from anxiety,
My mind from despair.
Deliver me from isolation,
My heart from loneliness.
Deliver me from fearfulness,
And keep me from wastefulness.
Deliver me from all that would disturb,
And enfold me in your peace.
Come, Lord, surround me with your light,
Keep me under your protecting love.
Strengthen me with your gracious power,
My strong deliverer and my Saviour.

FRUITLESS JOURNEY

Why have I travelled so far,
When what I seek is within my heart?
Why have I searched the earth,
When the God I seek is within me?
Why have I collected words,
When the Word is made flesh before me?
Why have I collected crumbs,
While ignoring the bread of life?
Like a vagrant, I pick up scraps of ideas,
While the Mighty God fills my being.
I have collected and pressed dead flowers,
While all of life flows and moves about me.
Come, my Lord, awaken me to life,
Open my eyes to your glory,
Open my heart to your love.

RESTORE MY VISION

Let there be a gleam in my eye again, O Lord,
For my sight is growing dim.
All around me lacks glory,
The world is dull and grey.
Restore my vision, open my eyes,
Keep me from the kingdom of the blind.
Let me not be among the walking dead.
Touch my heart, that it may warm
To the wonders and beauty of the day.
Be at one with me, O mighty Lord,
Make this the place of my resurrection,
A place of new vision and new hope.
Let not the evil ones prevail, O Lord.
Let no one rejoice because I am down.

Lord, I am shattered to the roots,
I have lost all identity and purpose.
Yet somewhere within is a light,
For you are at the centre of my life:
You are in the heart of the world.
Lord, I trust your light and love.
When this heaviness is gone,
Let my heart rejoice again in you,
And sing of your mercy and love.

WE WHO ARE PERISHABLE

We who are perishable,
Call upon the eternal.

We who are weak,
Call upon the Almighty.

We who are weary,
Call upon the Life-giver.

We who are foolish,
Call upon the Fount of Wisdom.

We who are lost,
Call upon him who is the Way.

We who are sinful,
Call upon the forgiving One.

We who are mortal,
Call upon the Immortal.

HAVE MERCY ON ME

Have mercy.
Have mercy on me, a sinner.

Lord, Jesus Christ, Son of God,
Grant us your grace,
Guide us in all goodness,
Give us a glimpse of glory:
    Have mercy.
    Have mercy on me, a sinner.

Lord, Jesus Christ, Son of God,
Your protection be about me,
Your peace be within me,
Your presence be ever with me:
    Have mercy.
    Have mercy on me, a sinner.

Lord, Jesus Christ, Son of God,
Your love to enfold me,
Your light to surround me,
Your life to redeem me:
    Have mercy.
    Have mercy on me, a sinner.

Lord Jesus, Christ, Son of God,
In times of storm and distress,
In times of fear and darkness,
In times of danger and weakness:
    Have mercy.
    Have mercy on me, a sinner.

Lord, Jesus Christ, Son of God:
    Have mercy.
    Have mercy on me, a sinner.

LET US NOT BE LOST

Those who have lost their senses say, 'There is no God.'
They have lost all feeling of awe and wonder,
They are untouched by beauty, unmoved by mystery.
They have become unaware of the holy, the totally other.
Narrowing the world to their own blindness of vision,
They cannot see beyond the limits of their own self.
Losing God, they have lost all sense of goodness,
Everything becomes relative to what they want and desire.
No one pursues grace or generosity, no not one.
To deny God's love and care is the depths of insensitivity.
This comes from the heart when the heart has turned to stone.

Come, Lord, renew and refresh your people.
Create a new heart within us.
Enlarge our vision, extend our sight,
Make us sensitive to each other and to you.
Come, Lord, be our refuge and strength in this time of trouble.

HELP US TO TURN

Lord, every day we travel,
We move forwards or backwards.
We journey deeper into your kingdom,
Or we turn our face towards hell.
Each action takes us towards the light,
Or plunges us into greater darkness.
Grant that we may be single-minded,
For there can be no double-dealing with you.
Help us, Lord, to turn our hearts toward you,
Prevent us from turning in on ourselves.
Grant that our relationship with you
Will enrich all our relationships.
As you give us your love and yourself,
May we give ourselves and love to others.
Open our eyes to the beauty about us,
Our minds and hearts to wonder and awe,
That we may walk in your presence,
And never stray from your way.
May we return to you, loving God,
Knowing that our sins are forgiven,
And that you welcome us home.

ASYLUM SEEKER

Lord, I am an asylum seeker,
I come for your protection and peace.
I ask you to accept me into your kingdom.
Without you, my Lord, I am nothing,
If I lose you, my world falls apart.
I would come to you and your love.
Show me your grace and your almighty power.
Without you, my Lord, I would return to the dust,
To the nothingness out of which you made me.
I know in my heart you created me out of love,
I was shaped out of your very own being,
You formed me for yourself and your love.
Lord, I belong to you, my Maker and Lover,
In turning to you and your love, I find you waiting.
To return to you and face you is homecoming,
I know that I am safe and accepted at last.
In you, Lord, my heart rejoices,
My mind, body and whole being rest secure.
You will not let me stay in the darkness of hell,
You will lift me up from the depths of the earth.
In your love, I will rise above what would keep me down,
I will come to rejoice in the fullness of life.
I will know that you are my God and Father,
By your grace, I will be known as an inheritor of your kingdom.

SILENCE

O God, I struggle, how I struggle.
I want to believe, I want to love you.
I ask what you want me to do, what is your will,
But I am not sure that there is an answer.
I keep silent, making room for you to speak,
The silence is empty and painful.
Others seem to know what you require of me,
But I do not have the first clue, not one inkling.
How do I know that I do have a vocation
If I do not hear your voice, not even a whisper?
Yet, I know that you created me out of your love.
I believe you have a purpose for me, I am here for a reason.
Your love is revealed all around me, in your creation.
Your presence is a comfort and strength at all times.
I look forward to the day when I behold your glory,
The time when I am fully aware of you.
Lord, teach me that I dwell in you always.
I could never live for a moment outside your presence.
Lord, teach me the secret of your indwelling,
That I may abide in you and you in me.
Let me rest in your heart, O gracious God,
And let my heart overflow with your presence.

IN WEAKNESS I COME

O God, I am sick of my illness:
It makes me think too much about myself.
I concentrate too much on my own being.
It is not good to be so egocentric.
There are times when hell confronts me:
Death seeks to be my companion.
Wanton destruction seeks to overwhelm me.
I put up my shutters and seek safety:
I hide and look for comfort and help.
You, O God, are my strength, my health:
You, O Lord, are my salvation.

I trust in you, my rock and my fortress,
Mighty deliverer in times of trouble.
In weakness I come to your power.
I bring my foolishness to your great wisdom.
In my confusion and distress I look for your guidance.
You, O God, are my strength, my health:
You, O Lord, are my salvation.

I turn to you, O Lord, in hope and in faith:
Come, Lord, enfold me in your love.
You are the power of my life, in you I arise.
I come from your love, I return to your love.
You, dear God, have reached down from on high:
You have rescued me in your Son, Jesus Christ.
You, O God, are my strength, my health:
You, O Lord, are my salvation.

Let me know that this breaking down is for rebuilding.
In you I am to be strengthened, renewed and restored:
You are the Lord making all things new.
Renew us, O God, and restore us.
Restore our peace and our joy in living.
Restore our health and our fullness of life.
Restore our faith and heal our blindness.

Restore our trust and our confidence in you.
Change us, O Lord, and we shall be changed.
You, O God, are my strength, my health:
You, O Lord, are my salvation.

COME, RENEW US

Come, Lord, come to us.
Enter our darkness with your light,
Fill our emptiness with your presence,
Come refresh, restore, renew us.
In our sadness, come as joy,
In our troubles, come as peace,
In our fearfulness, come as hope,
In our darkness, come as light,
In our frailty, come as strength,
In our loneliness come as love,
Come refresh, restore, renew us.

Straying

STRAYING

Some went astray in desert wastes
and found no path to a city to dwell in.
Hungry and thirsty, their soul was fainting within them,
So they cried to the Lord in their trouble
and he delivered them from their distress.

Psalm 107.4–6

WHERE ARE YOU, LORD?

Lord, why do you keep silent?
Where are you when I am troubled?
I see the wicked triumph every day:
I hurt for the pain of the poor.
The greedy gain and go forward:
Even the evil are seen to enjoy life.
So often the saintly meet suffering:
The good get no gratitude or gain.
Where are you, Lord my God?
I need to know your tender care.

I am with you always:
I never leave you, I abide with you.
In this world evil has freedom:
The wicked choose their way.
They may hurt, cheat and destroy:
But they cannot gain the victory.
They may win round after round:
But the final victory is yours.
In me, you are more than conquerors:
In me you have eternal life.
In the silence know I am Almighty:
I am with you now and forever.

SAVIOUR OF THE SINFUL

Saviour of the sinful,
Need of the needy,
Help of the helpless,
Hope of the hopeless,
Strength of the weak,
Healer of the sick,
Love of the loveless,
Come, O Christ.

LEAD ME, LORD

I am in trouble: Lord, hear me.
I am distressed in body and mind.
Listen to me, Lord of lords,
Hear my heartfelt cry, my prayer from the depths.
In my desperation I call upon you for survival.
In my great trouble I turn to you, God Almighty.
Lead me, Lord, go ahead of me.
Drive away my fears and my enemy.
Lord, make my way smooth and straight,
Until I recover my strength and my confidence.
Give me joy this day for my journeying.
Lord, let all who call upon you find you.
Be to all a mighty strength and shield.
Forgive us our sinfulness and wandering.
We have left your way for confusion and darkness.
We have turned from your path and into trouble.
We have brought upon ourselves pain and distress.
Our wounds are self-inflicted, for you would not hurt us.
Lord, hear our cry, forgive our sins, cleanse and restore us.
Holy God, listen to our plea and be our leader and guide.

I AM UNSURE

Lord, I am unsure:
The future is all unknown.
I do not know what to do,
Or what lies before me.
Let me know who is there.
Let me know you are here.

I do not know what will happen:
I cannot predict my path.
I often walk in the darkness,
I cannot see what is ahead.
Let me know who is there.
Let me know you are here.

I do not know where I shall go:
I am unsure of the road.
I do not know much of tomorrow,
Yet I know you and your love.
I know you will meet me there.

I am uncertain of the way:
I do not know where I am to travel,
I am so able to get lost.
Yet you are there as my guide.
I know you will meet me there.

I do not know how life will treat me:
I do not know if friends will leave me,
Or if health and strength will fail me.
Yet I can depend on you and your love.
I know you will meet me there.

I AM A WRECK

O Lord,
I am in ruins, restore me.
I am distressed, give me peace.
I am walking in the darkness,
Draw me again to your light.
I am afraid your glory will blind me,
Lord, protect me by your love.
Let me know you are watching,
And wanting me to return.
You wait with open arms
To welcome me home.
Forgive me, Father, I have sinned.
I feel like a long-lost sheep,
I have erred and strayed far away.
Let me hear your voice calling me,
The voice that calls me by my name.
Lord, you are my strength and my salvation,
You are the hope and joy of my life.
Lord, I will come to you soon,
Give me courage and strength to return.

saved

SAVED

The Lord is my light and my salvation;
whom then shall I fear?
The Lord is the strength of my life;
of whom then shall I be afraid?

Psalm 27.1

SING HIS PRAISES

In my darkness I waited upon the Lord:
He came down to me to support me.
He arose and lifted me up out of hell:
He gave his presence as light.
He set my feet on firm ground:
He went before me to guide me.
He led me out of the land of shadows:
He brought me to radiant life.
It is God that puts a song in my heart:
He lightens my journeying with his love.
New praises issue out of my mouth:
Blessed are all they that trust in him.
Blessed are they who know his presence:
Who are aware of his abundant mercy.
Rejoice all who know his saving power:
Sing praises to your God and deliverer.
Say and sing with me, 'Great is the Lord:
Wonderful is the love of the Almighty.'

AN EVENING BLESSING

Loving Lord, bless this place:
Let your love be here.
Fill it with your peace:
Let your joy be here.
Fill it with your grace:
Let your light be here.
Fill it with your power:
Let your presence be here.
Fill us with the knowledge
That you are here.

LISTEN

Lord, hear me when I call.
In your love and mercy hear my prayer.
Out of the depths of my being I cry.
Lord, please listen to me.

O mortal, my ear is always tuned to hear.
My hand is ready to help you in your need.
My power is offered to you in your weakness.
My bright light will enter your deep darkness.
My loving heart is ever open to your cry.
Listen, for I call and seek you out in love.

Now, Lord, I can rest in peace.
I can lie down in safety and in faith.
For nothing can separate me from your love,
The love revealed in Christ my Saviour.

IN GOD

Let me know that I am in the heart of God,
That I may rejoice in him.
Let me know that I am in the love of God,
That I may live in him.
Let me know that I am in the peace of God,
That I may rest in him.
Let me know that I am in the power of God,
That I may venture through him.

Teach me that God is in my heart,
That I may seek him.
Teach me that God is within me,
That I may talk to him.
Teach me that God dwells in me,
That I may love him.

Lord, I rejoice in your indwelling.
I am secure, for I dwell in you.
I have peace, for you dwell in me.
May I abide in you forever.

AFFIRMATIONS

I am in the presence of
The Father who created me.
I am in the presence of
The Son who redeemed me.
I am in the presence of
The Spirit who guides me.
In love and adoration.

I rejoice in the Creator,
Maker of heaven and earth.
I rejoice in the Saviour,
Who is of lowly birth.
I rejoice in the Spirit,
Giving life its worth.
In love and adoration.

I call upon the Father,
To strengthen and uphold me.
I call upon the Son,
To forgive and to shield me.
I call upon the Spirit,
To comfort and direct me.
In love and adoration.

I rest in the love,
Of the glorious Father.
I rest in the love,
Of the wonderful Saviour.
I rest in the love,
Of the blessed Spirit.
In love and adoration.
Today and forever,
In love and adoration.

LORD OF JOY

You, Lord, are here, in this place.
Your presence fills it,
Your presence is joy.

Lord of joy,
Open our eyes to see your beauty,
That we may delight in your creation.
Open our ears to hear your call,
That we may take pleasure in serving you.

Lord of joy,
Touch our hearts with your love,
That we may be alert to your desire for us.
Awaken us this day to behold your glory,
That we may be aware of your presence.

Lord of joy,
Touch our dull eyes,
That they may see beyond the obvious.
Touch our deafened ears,
That they may hear the still small voice.

Lord of joy,
This day protect us from evil,
Guide us in our journeying,
Keep us from all harm,
That we may rejoice in your love and protection.

O GOD, MAKE SPEED TO SAVE US

O God, make speed to save us.
O Lord, make haste to help us.
With trouble all around:
O God, make speed to save us.
All our foes confound:
O Lord, make haste to help us.
In our sore distress:
O God, make speed to save us.
In the time of fearfulness:
O Lord, make haste to help us.
Grant us, Lord, your peace:
O God, make speed to save us.
From our sins release:
O Lord, make haste to help us.
When we shed a tear:
O God, make speed to save us.
Let your presence be near:
O Lord, make haste to help us.
As in days of old:
O God, make speed to save us.
Your love and peace unfold:
O Lord, make haste to help us.

LORD, BEAR US UP

Lord, bear us up, as an eagle carries her young,
Lift us on high with the power of your wings.
Lord, if you raise us up we shall never die.
Lift us when all is pain and strife,
Lift us in the sorrows of our life.
In the hurting of the heart,
When relationships are torn apart.
In the shattering of our dreams,
When nothing is as it really seems.
Lord, every time we stumble and fall,
Come to our aid, on you we call.

Let us know that love conquers hate,
Faith triumphs over what we call fate.
Let us see your light dispels the night,
You can make our darkness bright.
Lord, bear us up, as on eagle's wings,
Lift us high until our heart sings,
Sings of you and of your deep love,
Sings of your power and help from above.

ENFOLD US IN YOUR PEACE

When the storms increase,
Keep us, Lord, in your care:
Enfold us in your peace.

In the madness of the mind,
In the follies of humankind:
Enfold us in your peace.

In the storms of our spirit,
In the weakness we inherit:
Enfold us in your peace.

In the troubles of the heart,
In all that would tear us apart:
Enfold us in your peace.

In the breakdown of relations,
In the warring of the nations:
Enfold us in your peace.

When we know we cannot cope,
When we give up all hope:
Enfold us in your peace.

When we feel we are going mad,
When everything seems bad:
Enfold us in your peace.

When all around is full of strife,
When we lose our grip on life:
Enfold us in your peace.

LORD, IN YOU WE LIVE

Lord, in you I live and move: I cannot fall out of your love.
I am always in your presence: I am never far from your peace.
Wherever I wander, you are there to greet me.
If I travel far overseas you are still there to meet me.
When my life enters into trouble, you desire to help me.
When I soar with joy and elation, you seek to share with me.
You are always there, you never leave or forsake me.
I can ignore or reject you, yet you are ready to accept me.
I can forget you and turn away, yet you patiently seek me.
When I lose my grasp of you, with a firm grip you hold me.
If I fall and am down, in mighty power you raise me.

Open my eyes to your glory and fill my heart with your presence.
Let me make spaces in my day and life for you to enter.
Grant that I may find you in the depth of my being.
Lord, ever present, you wait upon me to invite you to share my
   life.
Come Lord, come in light and love.
Come Lord, come in power and peace.
Come, dear Lord, fill me and make me aware of you.

GOD OF LOVE

God of love and gentleness,
Protect us by your goodness,
From each act of sinfulness,
From each deed of carelessness,
From each word of hurtfulness,
From each thought of wickedness.
By your presence and your holiness,
God of love and gentleness,
Protect us by your goodness.

BEYOND WORDS

No one can describe your beauty,
No one can tell of your power.
No words can capture your glory,
You cannot be pressed like a flower.
The mind cannot grasp or understand
Your mysteries or your might.
Yet what the brain cannot hold,
You allow our heart to contain.
We seek you with all our being,
While we dwell in your presence.
As we search and search for you,
You fill our days, our lives and hearts.
We are in your presence, peace and power,
Let us rest in you this day and always.

IN GOD'S HANDS

I rejoice in the hands of God,
Today, tomorrow and forever.
I am ever in the hands of God,
Powerful hands to support me,
Gentle hands to uphold me,
Peaceful hands to calm me,
Guiding hands to lead me,
Loving hands to enfold me,
Healing hands to strengthen me,
Saving hands to rescue me,
Redeeming hands to save me,
Graceful hands to accept me.
I rejoice in the hands of God,
Today, tomorrow and forever.

TODAY YOU BLESS US

Today you bless us, Lord,
Today, tomorrow, and always.
With the sun's brightness,
The rain's gentleness,
The snow's whiteness.
Today you bless us, Lord,
Today, tomorrow, and always.
With the earth's goodness,
With the water's pureness,
With the air's freshness.

Today you bless us, Lord,
Today, tomorrow, and always.
With our friend's faithfulness,
With our loved one's kindness,
With your own holiness.

Today you bless us, Lord,
Today, tomorrow, and always.
With strength for our work,
Light for our way,
Peace for our mind,
Power for this day,
Presence with us now,
Love for always.

WHAT ARE WE?

What are we humans, that you care for us?
A mere breath inspired with the breath of God,
Made of clay containing the divine love,
An earthen vessel, holding great treasure,
A limited edition, destined for eternity,
Frail flesh full of the Almighty.
Born of this earth, made for heaven,
Owning nothing, yet heirs to the kingdom.
Created out of love and for you eternally.

REST AT THE LAST

When the storms of the mind are over,
When the wave's last surge is done,
Lord, let me enter into your peace.
Come, meet me on the shore.
After the very last breath I take,
Come, Lord, rescue me from death.
When in deep sleep my eyelids close,
Lord, awaken me and let me rise.
Lord, let me rejoice with you,
And abide in your kingdom forever.

In the presence of the Holy One,
In the glory of Christ the Son,
In the power of the Holy Spirit,
In the love of the sacred Trinity,
Lord, let me rejoice with you,
And abide in your kingdom forever.

I ARISE IN GOD

I arise today,
In the strength of the Creator,
Who shaped the earth,
The Maker of sun and moon,
The designer of the stars,
In the power of the Almighty.

I arise today,
In the strength of the Saviour,
In the might of his crucifixion,
In the joy of his resurrection,
In the glory of his ascension,
In the power of the Redeemer.

I arise today,
In the fellowship of the Spirit,
In his guidance and direction,
In his wisdom and life giving,
In his renewing and restoring,
In the power of the Sanctifier.

I arise today,
In the mystery of the Trinity,
God's might to uphold me,
Christ's love to enfold me,
The Spirit's grace to guide me.

I arise today,
In the power of the Trinity.
I worship the unity,
I praise the diversity.
I arise today,
In the presence of the Holy Three.
I rejoice in the Trinity.

THE LORD IS SURE

The Lord is sure and will keep us,
The Lord gives us faith, hope and love.

The love that is fickle,
Have no faith in.
The hope that is halting,
Have no hand in.
The faith that falters,
Have no footing in.
For these will ebb,
As they flow.

Love the Lord,
The loyal One.
Hope in the Lord,
The Holy One.
Have faith in the Lord,
The faultless One.
He with you will abide,
Whatever the tide.

THE HEART OF GOD

I am in the heart of God,
I abide in his love,
I rest in his peace,
I rejoice in his power,
I walk under his protection.

I am in the heart of God,
Ever in his presence,
Always in his heart.

His wisdom guides me,
His grace goes with me,
His strength supports me,
His love sustains me,
God is in my heart.

I am in the heart of God,
Ever in his presence,
Always in his heart.

God is in the heart
Of loved one and stranger,
Of every living creature,
Of his whole universe,
God is in the heart.

I am in the heart of God,
Ever in his presence,
Always in his heart.

Nothing can separate us
From the love of God.
His love, filling all things,
Is waiting to be revealed
To all who look for him.

I am in the heart of God,
Ever in his presence,
Always in his heart.

AWARENESS OF GOD

Happy are they who know the Lord as their God,
Who are aware of his glory,
Those who delight in the presence of the Almighty,
Who meditate on his love day and night.
They have a stability that cannot be taken from them,
A sure haven in times of storm and trouble.
In the Lord they are more than conquerors,
In him they triumph over adversity.
They are a people with a future,
With a life that has no end.
Like a tree planted by life-giving water,
They will survive in times of drought.
Life lived in awareness of God
Is a life of purpose and of reality.
The godless have no sure stability,
They chase after false securities.
They are a mere breath that passes,
They have no real place of rest,
And no hope of eternal life.
When the storms arise and the wind blows,
They blow away and are no more to be seen.
Our home is with the everlasting Father,
Our future is to move towards the glory of eternity.

HELP ME TO COPE

Open my eyes, that I sleep not in death,
Inspire me by your Spirit with every breath.
Touch my heart with the fire of your love,
Let my whole life burn with fire from above.
Guide my feet in your straight and narrow way,
Strengthen my will, that I do not stray.
I need you, Lord, I need your great might,
I need your protection, by day and by night.
Here is my heart, here is my hope,
Lord, never depart, help me to cope.
Here is my mind, here is my will,
Lord, peaceful and kind, help me be still.

GOD BE WITH US

All this day,
God be with us. Amen.

In all our work,
In rest and play,
God be with us. Amen.

In every meeting,
As life unravels,
God be with us. Amen.

In every greeting,
And in the light,
God be with us. Amen.

In the deep darkness,
In every night,
God be with us. Amen.

In every sorrow,
And every joy,
God be with us. Amen.

In each moment,
And every hour,
God be with us. Amen.

All this day,
And tomorrow,
God be with us. Amen.

HOLDING THE ALMIGHTY

The infinite is held by the finite.
The incomprehensible is grasped by the heart.
That which heaven cannot contain is held in human hands.
The God beyond our reach is touched.
He who is beyond our sight is seen among us.
This wonder is hard to believe,
The mind cannot take it in,
The Word is made flesh and dwelling among us.

Heaven and earth are one in him,
Our God has come among us.
He comes to share in our humanity,
That we may partake of his divinity.
Let us be humble before this mystery,
Bow before him who is the Lord.
This little child, held in Mary's arms,
Is the Christ, our Lord and our Saviour.

GOD WITH YOU

The presence of the sacred Three,
The blessing of the Trinity,
Be upon your working day,
Upon the people on your way,
Upon your labour and your toil,
Upon the earth and the soil,
Upon the tools that you take,
Upon the things that you make,
Upon the thoughts of your mind,
Upon your sharing with humankind,
Upon the love that you share,
Upon all for whom you care.
The presence of the sacred Three,
The blessing of the Trinity.

CALLED BY GOD

You have called my name,
In the night, across the years.
You have called again and again,
In my joy and my tears.
The words, never quite the same,
Seeking out my dulled ears,
Calling me to awake and rise,
And to cast aside all my fears.

More than this, I should know,
When the day is turned to night,
And wherever I go you are there,
Drawing me into your light,
Seeking me at my last breath,
Calling me to rise from death.

Seasonal

SEASONAL

I will sing of your strength
and every morning praise your steadfast love;
For you have been my stronghold, my refuge in the day of trouble.
To you, O my strength, will I sing;
For you, God, are my refuge and my steadfast love.

Psalm 59.16–17

DIVINE PRAISES

Blessed are you, Lord God, King of the universe,
Prince of peace, to you be praise and glory forever.
Your coming gives new hopes to our lives.
Your coming lightens our darkness,
Strengthens us in our weakness,
Brings peace to our troubles,
And comfort in our distress.
Lord, fill our lives,
With your love,
With your light,
With your life,
That we may live to praise and glorify you.
Blessed are you, God, now and forever.

COME AND CHANGE US

Come, Lord, come.
Come and change us.
Convince,
Convert,
Consecrate.
Come, Lord, come.
Come and change us.

Return, Lord, return.
Return and revive us.
Renew,
Refresh,
Restore.
Return, Lord, return.
Return and revive us.

ADVENT ANTHEM

Come Lord,
Come down, come in, come among us.

Come, O Wisdom of God,
Enlighten our minds, destroy the darkness of our ignorance.
Come Lord,
Come down, come in, come among us.

Come, O Lord of lords,
In you alone is our peace. Rule in our hearts and homes.
Come Lord,
Come down, come in, come among us.

Come, O Root of Jesse,
Promised Saviour, let us share in your redeemed humanity.
Come Lord,
Come down, come in, come among us.

Come, O Key of David,
Close to us all that would hurt us. Open for us the kingdom of
    heaven.
Come Lord,
Come down, come in, come among us.

Come, O Morning Star,
Herald of the new day. Give light to us, and to all who are in
    darkness.
Come Lord,
Come down, come in, come among us.

Come, O Desire of the Nations,
We look for you. We long for you. Grant us true justice and
    peace.
Come Lord,
Come down, come in, come among us.

Come, O Emmanuel,
God ever present. Make us aware of you and your eternal love.
Come Lord,
Come down, come in, come among us.

WISDOM OF GOD

Come, Wisdom of God.
Come, Christ our Lord.

Come from the depth of your glory,
Fill us with your radiance and transform us.
Come, Wisdom of God.
Come, Christ our Lord.

Come from the depth of your power,
Enter into our confusion and direct us.
Come, Wisdom of God.
Come, Christ our Lord.

Come from the depth of your love,
Enter our hearts and enliven us.
Come, Wisdom of God.
Come, Christ our Lord.

Come from the depth of your light,
Enter our dullness and enlighten us.
Come, Wisdom of God.
Come, Christ our Lord.

Wisdom of God there at the beginning,
Come, refresh and restore us.
Come, Wisdom of God.
Come, Christ our Lord.

LORD OF LORDS

Come, Lord of lords.
Come, Christ Jesus.

Ruler of your people,
Giver of peace and prosperity.
Come, Lord of lords.
Come, Christ Jesus.

Lord of the burning bush,
Revealed through your creation.
Come, Lord of lords.
Come, Christ Jesus.

Lord of the desert,
Be our guide and our protector.
Come, Lord of lords.
Come, Christ Jesus.

Lord of the living water,
Refresh and revive your people.
Come, Lord of lords.
Come, Christ Jesus.

Lord of the manna in the wilderness,
Sustain us in our journey through life.
Come, Lord of lords.
Come, Christ Jesus.

Lord, the lawgiver of Mount Sinai,
We seek your will and obey you.
Come, Lord of lords.
Come, Christ Jesus.

Lord, our Redeemer and Saviour,
We need your strength and your power.
Come, Lord of lords.
Come, Christ Jesus.

THE ROOT OF JESSE

Jesus, Word made flesh,
Dwelling among us,
Maranatha:
Come, Christ our Lord.

Jesus, of the House of David,
Sharing in our human form,
Maranatha:
Come, Christ our Lord.

Jesus, Son of the Virgin Mary,
Aware of our joys and sorrows,
Maranatha:
Come, Christ our Lord.

Jesus, born as a child in a stable,
Yet King of kings and Lord of lords,
Maranatha:
Come, Christ our Lord.

Jesus, fleeing as a refugee,
Yet ruler of heaven and earth,
Maranatha:
Come, Christ our Lord.

Jesus, from your throne in majesty,
From the realms of your glory,
Maranatha:
Come, Christ our Lord.

THE KEY OF DAVID

Jesus our Redeemer,
Come, set your people free.

Lord, you hold the key to life,
You open to us the way to eternity.
Jesus our Redeemer,
Come, set your people free.

You alone can loose us from our sins,
You can lead us into glorious liberty.
Jesus our Redeemer,
Come, set your people free.

You are our mighty Saviour,
Born of the House of David.
Jesus our Redeemer,
Come, set your people free.

Holy and Strong One,
We bring to you the troubles and needs of nations.
Jesus our Redeemer,
Come, set your people free.

We rejoice in you, God Almighty,
You have opened the kingdom of heaven to all believers.
Jesus our Redeemer,
Come, set your people free.

THE MORNING STAR

Maranatha:
Come, lighten our darkness.

Jesus is the Morning Star,
Risen to dispel our darkness.
Maranatha:
Come, lighten our darkness.

Come, Light of lights,
Dispel the darkness within and about us.
Maranatha:
Come, lighten our darkness.

Come, hope of glory,
Chase away all gloom and despair.
Maranatha:
Come, lighten our darkness.

Come, reveal to us your life,
And death's dark shadows put to flight.
Maranatha:
Come, lighten our darkness.

Come, shine upon us,
And open to us everlasting day.
Maranatha:
Come, lighten our darkness.

THE DESIRE OF THE NATIONS

In joyful expectation of his coming,
We pray to Jesus, the promised one.
Lord, we look for you.
We long for you.

Come to your church, Lord.
We watch for you. We wait for you.
Lord, we look for you.
We long for you.

O Desire of the nations,
May the all kingdoms of the world be your kingdom.
Lord, we look for you.
We long for you.

Come to your people who long for peace,
To all who cry out for justice.
Lord, we look for you.
We long for you.

Come to all who are lonely and look for love,
To all who long for your presence.
Lord, we look for you.
We long for you.

Come, in your power and glory,
And make us a people for your own.
Lord, we look for you.
We long for you.

O COME, EMMANUEL

O come, Emmanuel,
Be known among us.

Come, Lord, touch our eyes,
And we shall behold your glory.
O come, Emmanuel,
Be known among us.

Come, Lord, touch our ears,
And they shall hear your call.
O come, Emmanuel,
Be known among us.

Come, Lord, touch our lips,
And they shall sing your praises.
O come, Emmanuel,
Be known among us.

Come, Lord, touch our hearts,
And they shall fill with your love.
O come, Emmanuel,
Be known among us.

Come, Lord, touch our lives,
And we shall live and work for you.
O come, Emmanuel,
Be known among us.

Come, Lord, touch your people,
And set them free to worship you.
O come, Emmanuel,
Be known among us.

CHRIST INCARNATE

Christ, present at the beginning of creation:
We worship and adore you.
Christ, promised by the prophets:
We worship and adore you.
Christ, only Son of the Father:
We worship and adore you.
Christ, proclaimed by the angels:
We worship and adore you.
Christ, born of the Virgin Mary:
We worship and adore you.
Christ, protected by Joseph:
We worship and adore you.
Christ, worshipped by the shepherds:
We worship and adore you.
Christ, visited by the wise men:
We worship and adore you.
Christ, baptized in the Jordan:
We worship and adore you.
Christ, sharing in our humanity:
We worship and adore you.
Christ, turning water into wine:
We worship and adore you.
Christ, offering us your divinity:
We worship and adore you.
Christ, light of the world:
We worship and adore you.
Christ, conquering the darkness:
We worship and adore you.

Christ, a refugee in Egypt:
Have mercy upon us.
Christ, working in Nazareth:
Have mercy upon us.
Christ, in an earthly home:
Have mercy upon us.

Christ, healer of the sick:
Have mercy upon us.
Christ, lover of the poor:
Have mercy upon us.
Christ, lifter of the fallen:
Have mercy upon us.
Christ, protector of the weak:
Have mercy upon us.
Christ, hope of all the world:
Have mercy upon us.

SON OF GOD, HEAR US

Son of God, hear us.
Son of God, have mercy upon us.

Eternally begotten,
Son of the Father,
Word before all creation,
Revealing the Godhead,
Radiant in glory,
The Alpha and the Omega.
 Son of God, hear us.
 Son of God, have mercy upon us.

Bright Morning Star,
Sun of righteousness,
Light that no darkness can quench,
High priest in heaven,
Ever making intercession for us,
Our Light and our Salvation.
 Son of God, hear us.
 Son of God, have mercy upon us.

JESUS, SON OF MARY

Jesus, Son of Mary,
Have mercy upon us.

Grant us your peace,
Be with us and about us.
Jesus, Son of Mary,
Have mercy upon us.

Come in your great love,
Be within us and around us.
Jesus, Son of Mary,
Have mercy upon us.

Keep us from sin,
Protect us from evil.
Jesus, Son of Mary,
Have mercy upon us.

Be with us in the dawning,
Be with us in the morning.
Jesus, Son of Mary,
Have mercy upon us.

Be with us in the light,
Stay with us in the dark.
Jesus, Son of Mary,
Have mercy upon us.

BROKEN FOR US

Lord, broken on the cross,
You were shattered for us.
We come to you:
For you alone can make us whole.

We come with all broken people,
Whose lives are shattered.
We come to you:
For you alone can make us whole.

We come with those suffering from
Broken relationships, broken promises,
Broken hopes, broken dreams, broken hearts.
We come to you:
For you alone can make us whole.

We come with those suffering from
Broken bodies, those who have suddenly taken ill,
The injured in accidents, the victims of violence,
With all who are in hospital or needing care at home.
We come to you:
For you alone can make us whole.

We come with all those suffering from
Broken minds, the deeply disturbed,
The distressed, the depressed, the suicidal.
We come to you:
For you alone can make us whole.

We come to you, shattered on the cross,
Broken for our healing.
You are the risen Lord, the giver of life,
You renew us and offer us life eternal.
We come to you:
For you alone can make us whole.

COMING TO THE CROSS

The closer we come to each other,
The closer we come to God,
The closer we come to the cross.
The closer we come to love,
The closer we come to God,
The closer we come to the cross.

The closer we come to knowing,
The closer we come to the cross.
The closer we come to loving,
The closer we come to the cross.
The closer we come to the heart of God,
The closer we come to the cross.
The closer we come to the resurrection,
The closer we come to the cross,
And the closer we come to eternal life.

ABIDE WITH US, RISEN LORD

Abide with us, risen Lord.
Abide with us today,
Abide with us in the brightness.
Abide with us in our strength,
Abide with us in our weakness.
Abide with us in our joys,
Abide with us in our sorrows.
Abide with us tonight,
Abide with us in the darkness.
Abide with us in life,
Abide with us in death.
Abide with us in time,
Abide with us for eternity.

RISEN LORD, LIFT US UP

By the power of your resurrection,
Risen Lord, lift us.
By your conquering of death,
Risen Lord, lift us.
By your triumph over the grave,
Risen Lord, lift us.
By your descending into hell,
Risen Lord, lift us.
By your appearing to Mary,
Risen Lord, lift us.
By your peace offered to the disciples,
Risen Lord, lift us.
By your abiding at Emmaus,
Risen Lord, lift us.
By your accepting of Thomas,
Risen Lord, lift us.
By your presence ever with us,
Risen Lord, lift us.

RISEN LORD

As the day dawns,
We rejoice that the Son is risen.
Christ, come to us.
Destroy the darkness of death,
Disperse the clouds of night,
Warm our hearts with your love,
Guide our travels with your light.
Let us walk with you,
As children of the day and not the night.
In your light, this day we shall see light.
We welcome you, giver of hope and life,
Conqueror of death and hell.
We rejoice in you and in eternal life.
Alleluia.

JESUS, HEAR US

Jesus, hear us.
Jesus, have mercy upon us.

Jesus, Word made flesh,
Jesus, proclaimed by the angels,
Jesus, born of the Virgin Mary,
Jesus, adored by the shepherds,
Jesus, worshipped by the wise men.
    Jesus, hear us.
    Jesus, have mercy upon us.

Jesus, turning water into wine,
Jesus, turning our poverty into riches,
Jesus, turning our sadness into joy,
Jesus, sharing in our humanity.
    Jesus, hear us.
    Jesus, have mercy upon us.

Jesus, scorned and rejected,
Jesus, crucified and buried,
Jesus, descending into hell,
Jesus, risen from the dead,
Jesus, with us always.
    Jesus, hear us.
    Jesus, have mercy upon us.

CHRIST, HEAR US

Christ, hear us.
Christ, have mercy upon us.

Christ, holy and blessed One,
Foretold of by the prophets,
Christ, our Messiah and Redeemer,
Sitting at the right hand of the Father.
    Christ, hear us.
    Christ, have mercy upon us.

Christ, our hope and our joy,
Filling our lives with light and love,
Christ, our peace and our perfecting,
Come as our Saviour and our Friend.
    Christ, hear us.
    Christ, have mercy upon us.

Christ, ascended into the heavens,
Making intercession to the Father,
Christ, light of lights and judge of all,
Bring us to glory of your kingdom.
    Christ, hear us.
    Christ, have mercy upon us.

FLAME OF THE SPIRIT

Flame of the Spirit,
Burn within us,
Set our hearts on fire,
And we shall be changed.

Wind of the Spirit,
Blow through us,
Move us by your power,
And we shall be changed.

Breath of God,
Fill our lives,
Inspire our actions,
And we shall be changed.

When the shutters are down and the doors closed,
Come. **Fill us, Holy Spirit.**
When we are dried up and all hope is gone,
Come. **Fill us, Holy Spirit.**
When chaos rules and we live in fear,
Come. **Fill us, Holy Spirit.**
When our resources are gone and we cannot cope,
Come. **Fill us, Holy Spirit.**
When we are restricted and it feels like the grave,
Come. **Fill us, Holy Spirit.**
Come inspire, refresh, renew us.

SPIRIT OF GOD

Holy and Mighty One,
Holy and Strong One:
May the power of your Spirit
Enable us.
May the brooding of your Spirit
Awaken us.
May the fire of your Spirit
Enflame us.
May the wind of your Spirit
Move us.
May the wisdom of your Spirit
Inspire us.
May the breath of your Spirit
Enliven us.
May the gifts of your Spirit
Equip us.
May the presence of your Spirit
Be ever with us.
Holy and Mighty One,
Holy and Strong One.

WELCOME IN GOD'S NAME

(A Baptismal Prayer)

In the presence of the Father,
In the peace of Christ the Son,
In the power of the Spirit:
The Holy Three and Blessed One.

In the light of God the Father,
In the love of Christ the Son,
In the leading of the Spirit:
The Holy Three and Blessed One.

In the goodness of the Father,
In the grace of Christ the Son,
In guidance of the Spirit:
The Holy Three and Blessed One.

In the strength of God the Father,
In the salvation of the Son,
In the sanctity of the Spirit:
The Holy Three and Blessed One.

We welcome you.

Let everything that has breath praise the Lord. Alleluia.
Psalm 150.6

MORE FROM DAVID ADAM

A Celtic Psaltery

David Adam has collected together in one volume some of the Celtic psalms that have inspired him. These songs for guidance or protection and prayers of thanksgiving can be used in public or private prayer.

Walking the Edges:
Living in the Presence of God

Reflecting on the stories of St Martin, St Cuthbert, St Patrick and others David Adam shows us what it means to be a saint. Above all it means having the courage and faith to step out of our comfort zones and being prepared to walk the edges in the presence of God.

A Desert in the Ocean:
God's Call to Adventurous Living

This meditation on a prayer attributed to the Celtic saint Brendan opens the way to an adventurous spirituality. Practical prayer exercises are included.

The Glory of Light
Island of Light
Landscapes of Light

Prayers by David Adam
with photographs by Robert Cooper

These three illustrated prayer books, combining stunning photographs of Holy Island with prayers by David Adam, would make beautiful gifts.

Landscapes of Light: 'one of the most beautiful prayer books I have come across for some considerable time'. (*New Link*)

For a full list of titles by David Adam, visit www.spck.org.uk

MORE FROM SPCK

For Love Alone
Mother Mary Agnes

Mother Mary Agnes continues the story of the religious community she founded on the Shetland island of Fetlar. Infused with Celtic spirituality, her writing displays the all-embracing love which is at the heart of their community life, while being firmly grounded in the daily events of this unique family.

This book follows *A Tide that Sings*, *The Song of the Lark* and *Island Song* which tell the story of the early days of the community.

Loved by Love:
Growing into Spiritual Health and Wholeness
Roy Williamson

Roy Williamson reflects on St Paul's great song of love, 1 Corinthians 13. These familiar words contain life-changing truths when taken seriously. 'In recent days,' the author writes, 'they have come to me with a freshness that is frightening and with a challenge that has rocked my status quo.' These reflections aim to help us choose, against the odds, the way of love, which puts the whole of life in perspective.

A Year of Grace:
365 Mealtime Prayers
William S. Kervin

An anthology of graces for every day of the year. The prayers, traditional and contemporary, come from around the world and reflect themes of thankfulness for creation, hospitality and friendship, the countryside and the seasons, and social justice.

Seasonal Worship from the Countryside
The Staffordshire Seven

Creative liturgies and prayers which draw on the traditions of rural worship. Connecting faith with the joys and trials of rural life, these resources can be used by churches in the country and in our towns and cities.

For a full list of SPCK titles, visit www.spck.org.uk